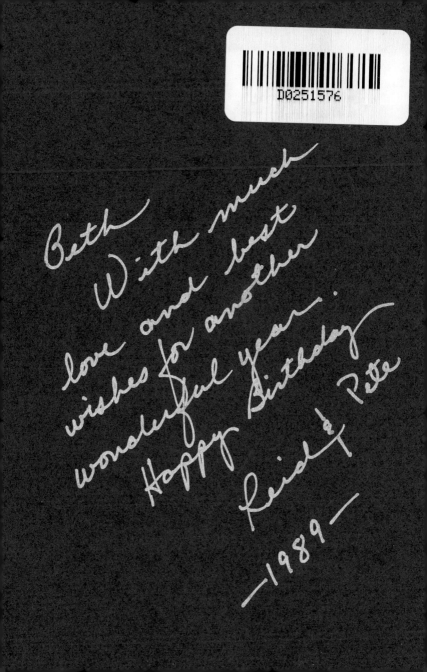

Beth

With much
love and best
wishes for another
wonderful year.

Happy Birthday

Heidi & Pete

—1989—

SOUFFLÉS

Happy Birthday,
Beth,
May your Soufflés
Soar. Best,
Ann

SOUFFLÉS

FORTY EASY
SAVORY AND SWEET
RECIPES —
FROM BAKED TO
FROZEN

ANN AMERNICK
AND RICHARD CHIROL

ILLUSTRATIONS BY SALLY STURMAN

Clarkson N. Potter, Inc./Publishers

DISTRIBUTED BY CROWN PUBLISHERS, INC.,

NEW YORK

Published by Clarkson N. Potter, Inc., 225 Park Avenue South,
New York, New York 10003

CLARKSON N. POTTER, POTTER, and colophon are
trademarks of Clarkson N. Potter, Inc.

Manufactured in the United States of America

Library of Congress Cataloging-in-Publication Data

Amernick, Ann.
Soufflés: forty easy savory and sweet recipes — from
baked to frozen.
Includes index.
1. Soufflés. I. Chirol, Richard. II. Title.
TX773.A42   1989   641.8′2   88–15173
ISBN 0-517-56978-7

Design by Jan Melchior

10 9 8 7 6 5 4 3 2 1

First Edition

For Morris

and

Helen Silverberg

ANN AMERNICK

For André Tranchant

and

Jean Marie Brossier

RICHARD CHIROL

CONTENTS

INTRODUCTION

Food writer and restaurateur George Lang, in his book *Lang's Compendium of Culinary Nonsense and Trivia*, tells the following soufflé story about the great chef Auguste Escoffier.

Once, when Escoffier did not know the exact timing of a dinner (because of the many courses involved and also because of speeches and other extenuating circumstances), he made ten different batches of soufflés, starting three minutes apart, to assure that one would be ready at just the right moment. The others were thrown out.

Producing a soufflé, bringing it to the table billowing prettily while dinner guests watch in wonderment, historically has been a project that only the most accomplished — and self-confident — cook would attempt.

Soufflés seem like magic; how else could these flavorful clouds be brought down to earth to be eaten by mere mortals? But magic is undependable as a kitchen technique. One day you might have it, the next day you might not.

Professional cooks, of course, have always known that it's not magic — that no matter how tricky the technique, if you use it over and over again every day for years, it becomes second nature.

But the home cook, who perhaps makes a soufflé once in a blue moon, never has a chance to master the technique. And while the process of producing a soufflé may become demystified after a while, it remains tedious. Especially vexing is the number of steps required.

Traditional soufflés are based on a mixture of flour and milk, which is boiled until thickened, technically the *bouilli*. Egg yolks are added to the *bouilli*, producing a thick custard. Then the egg whites are beaten and gently folded into the custard. In a French restaurant where we once worked, a veritable vat of *bouilli* was kept always at the ready, the better to accommodate the dessert rush.

But as it turns out, there is something new under the sun and that is what this book is all about. A brilliant and innovative Swiss chef, Fredy Girardet, discovered in the 1970s that the *bouilli* wasn't necessary. He found, in fact, that soufflés made without the *bouilli* were lighter in texture and more intense in flavor, which after all is the basic idea of the soufflé. So not only is there a bonus for cooks in Girardet's discovery but there's a bonus for the people who eat the soufflés as well.

It's these easier-to-make, lighter, more intensely fla-vored soufflés that are included in our book. Based only on beaten egg yolks and whites plus flavoring ingre-dients, our recipes take the intimidation factor out of making soufflés. These recipes have worked well for us as professional pastry chefs, and they have been care-fully tested in the home kitchen so that they'll work as well for you.

Our recipes for savory and sweet soufflés range from appetizers and hors d'oeuvres to main courses and des-serts. You'll find cream cheese and smoked salmon souf-flés that are perfect for brunch, cheese soufflés baked in special cream puffs that make wondrous lunch or supper dishes, and even some bite-size caviar soufflés for ele-gant appetizers. Among our desserts are frozen soufflés such as strawberry and grapefruit that can be prepared ahead, an intensely flavored chocolate-brownie soufflé, a maple-flavored soufflé baked in crêpes, plus others with interesting combinations of tastes.

UTENSILS

Whisks and mixers. The correct beating of egg whites is what makes or breaks (literally) your soufflé. You want to incorporate the maximum amount of air into the whites, but not beat them so long as to deflate them. Egg whites can be beaten with either the whisk attachment of an electric mixer (we prefer the Kitchen-aid heavy duty mixer) or a large, balloon-shaped wire whisk. The wire whisk is often the choice of professionals, who like the control it provides. Once you know the technique, beating by hand doesn't take any longer than doing it by machine, and the chances of overbeating are significantly less.

Bowls. The most efficient shape for beating eggs is a bowl with a round bottom and high sides. This shape provides maximum contact between whisk and eggs, and allows the eggs to be lifted instead of pushed around the sides of the bowl. A copper mixing bowl (for beating egg whites) is not by any means necessary, but many professional cooks and some of our scientific friends have found that, for obscure chemical reasons, egg whites whipped in a copper bowl will make your soufflé rise higher.

Rubber spatula. A flexible rubber spatula is invaluable for folding together soufflé ingredients.

Soufflé dishes. Soufflé dishes are available in ceramic

(we use Apilco make) or glass. They should be straight sided. In testing the recipes for this book, we considered a single-serving soufflé dish to be one that holds ¾ cup batter when filled to the top. One-cup molds can be used as well, but the baked soufflé won't puff much above the top rim and won't look so spectacular.

Some of the recipes also call for a 6-cup mold. An 8-cup size will work, but again, baked soufflés won't look as high and light.

Pastry bags. Professional cooks often pipe soufflé batter into baking dishes with a pastry bag. Less air is lost this way, the batter can be more evenly distributed, and there are less likely to be air pockets. Most of our soufflés can simply be spooned into prepared baking dishes, but a few, mainly those in which two colors of batter are alternated to make a fanciful design, do require a pastry bag. And two bags will make execution of these recipes even easier. There is no need to wash and dry the bag before you fill it again to pipe in the second color. Whether you buy one bag or two, you'll need a ¼-inch and a ½-inch tip for each. Most home cooks find the 10-inch or 12-inch bags the most useful and most workable.

Pastry brush. A brush is useful for spreading butter in the soufflé dish.

Citrus zester or fine grater. Several of our recipes depend on the intense fruity flavor of citrus zest — the colored part of the rind that adds flavor without the bitterness of the white pith. A citrus zester is a little implement that peels off tiny strips of the zest. It can be purchased in kitchenware shops. For tiny morsels of zest, use a fine grater.

Baking sheets and parchment paper. Baking sheets can be either flat cookie sheets or sheets with very low sides. Parchment paper is sometimes used on baking sheets and in cake pans to prevent baked goods from sticking. It is available in rolls in kitchenware and department stores. If you use nonstick bakeware, you won't need parchment paper.

Eight-inch frying or omelette pan. The pan should be ovenproof, preferably nonstick. If you want to try our souffléd omelettes, you've got to have one of these.

TIPS AND TECHNIQUES

Beating egg whites. Pay attention here, because this is the crux of soufflé-making. In order to get the fluffiest, puffiest soufflés, you must beat egg whites to their optimum point. The idea is to incorporate as much air as possible into the whites, but not to beat them so long that they break down and become lumpy. Aim for a smooth, creamy foam.

The recipes all use large eggs. Eggs should be at room temperature before you begin. Cold eggs can be warmed in the shell in warm water.

Try to avoid using your very freshest eggs for beaten egg whites. Some chefs prefer eggs that are a few weeks old because they produce a lighter, fluffier beaten white.

Start with a bowl and whisk that are scrupulously clean and perfectly dry. Any grease, bit of egg yolk, or moisture is likely to prevent the whites from reaching their maximum volume, or even from stiffening at all.

All the recipes call for the addition of a few drops of lemon juice to the whites before they are beaten. This acid helps stabilize the whites. In the sweet soufflés, sugar also enhances the stabilization. The sugar is added after the whites have been beaten just until foamy. Then it's added gradually while you continue beating.

The perfectly beaten egg white has very tiny bubbles, holds its shape when the whisk is lifted, and doesn't slide around the bowl. Beat past this point and you are likely to break down the molecules in the whites that are holding the air. Overbeaten whites look dull, become lumpy, and separate. You're more likely to get in trouble, in fact, if you overbeat rather than underbeat.

If you beat egg whites with a whisk, be sure to use a round-bottom bowl. Beat in circles perpendicular to the surface of the egg whites, lifting the whisk out of the whites at the highest point of the circle. If you're using a hand-held electric mixer, move the beaters around the sides of the bowl to produce the best result.

Beating egg yolks. In many but not all of these recipes, the egg yolks need to be beaten until they are very thick and light in color. Professionals use the term "ribbon" or "form a ribbon." This means that when the whisk is lifted from perfectly beaten yolks and moved horizontally above the surface, you'll be able to see a slowly dissolving "ribbon" on the surface of the yolks.

Folding. This is the technique you use to blend the egg whites with the other ingredients. Our recipes always call for the lighter ingredients (the beaten whites and whipped cream, if any) to be added to the heavier. The idea is to blend them without letting the heavier ingredients smash the air out of the tender lighter ingredients.

To fold, bring a rubber spatula down into the center of the mixture, across the bottom of the bowl and then up the side, rotating the spatula so that one edge is always in contact with the bowl. Repeat the motion, rotating the bowl slightly each time. Fold just until you no longer see streaks of separate ingredients.

Mixing order. In general, the egg yolks are beaten first, then the whites. Next, any other ingredients or flavorings are added to the yolks, and the whites are then folded into the yolk mixture. You may be tempted to switch the order of business around from time to time, but don't do it. This order is designed to get maximum volume and good looks from your soufflé batter.

Using fruit. A word about soufflés made with fruit. We encourage you to use fresh fruit as long as the flavor and texture enhance the recipe. Occasionally, however, depending on the time of year, we have found that canned fruits, such as apricots and pears, have a more reliable flavor.

Preparing soufflé dishes. Sweet soufflés are baked in buttered and sugared dishes. You need between ⅓ and ½ teaspoon butter and a teaspoon of sugar for each individual dish, and about 1½ teaspoons butter and 1½ table-spoons sugar for a 6- or 8-cup mold. Spread the softened butter very evenly all over the inside surface of the dish, including the rim; the best way to do this is with a pastry brush. Then very lightly, so as not to disturb the butter, sprinkle in the sugar and distribute it evenly by rotating the dish. Turn the dish upside down and shake lightly to empty out any excess sugar. Refrigerate the mold until ready to fill and bake. Soufflés rise better and will cook through without burning if they are put into cold molds. Molds manufactured for soufflés can go directly from refrigerator to oven.

Savory soufflés are baked in buttered dishes, while dishes for frozen soufflés receive no treatment at all.

Baking. All the recipes have been tested in a home oven with an accurate thermostat. Oven temperatures, how-ever, can sometimes vary by as much as 50 degrees from the temperatures indicated on the thermostat. Oven thermometers are often inaccurate as well. If you're unsure about the accuracy of your thermostat, you might want to have it tested. Local utility companies usually do this.

Most of our individual soufflés take only 8 to 10

minutes to bake, but those with fruit purées and a few others take slightly longer.

A perfectly baked soufflé is puffy and lightly browned on top, and slightly creamy inside. All baked soufflés need to be served immediately, since they begin to deflate within minutes of being removed from the oven.

Freezing. Frozen soufflés can be frozen in decorative molds as well as in regular soufflé dishes. To unmold, dip briefly in very hot water, then turn upside down on dessert plates.

BAKED

SAVORY

MUSTARD

SOUFFLÉS

CREAM CHEESE
AND SMOKED SALMON
SOUFFLÉ

This savory soufflé makes an interesting breakfast or brunch alternative to bagels with smoked salmon and cream cheese.

SERVES 4

2 tablespoons minced onions, or 1 tablespoon chopped chives

1 teaspoon unsalted butter

2 egg yolks

3 ounces cream cheese, at room temperature

1 tablespoon sour cream

1 tablespoon Dijon or Pommery mustard

2 ounces smoked salmon, finely chopped

4 egg whites

Few drops of lemon juice

Preheat the oven to 400° F.

Butter the insides of 4 individual soufflé molds and refrigerate.

If using onions, sauté in the butter until soft. Chives needn't be sautéed.

In a medium bowl, beat the egg yolks until very thick and light in color. Beat in the cream cheese, sour cream, mustard, and smoked salmon.

In another medium bowl, beat the egg whites with the lemon juice until firm but still glossy. Fold into the yolk mixture.

Spoon into prepared soufflé molds and bake for 8 to 10 minutes, or until puffy and browned on top.

HAM SOUFFLÉ
IN ROASTED RED
POTATOES

These tiny morsels, succulent and rich with smoked ham, make a wonderful appetizer. Pass them around on a large platter with plenty of napkins; guests will be happy to eat them with their fingers. If you want to use the leftover potato pulp, mash it with a little salt and pepper and a lightly beaten egg yolk, shape into small patties, and sauté in butter.

SERVES 6 AS AN APPETIZER

- **10 red new potatoes, about 2½ to 3 inches in diameter**
- **2 tablespoons (¼ stick) unsalted butter, melted**
- **2 egg yolks**
- **4 egg whites**
- **Few drops of lemon juice**
- **4 ounces smoked ham, finely chopped (see Note)**
- **2 teaspoons mustard (half-and-half Dijon and Pommery is perfect)**

½ teaspoon white pepper

Dash of Tabasco (optional)

Preheat the oven to 400° F.

Cut the potatoes in half and brush them all over with the melted butter. Place on a baking sheet and bake for about 30 minutes, or until tender. Let cool slightly, then scoop out most of the pulp, leaving shells about ¼ inch thick. Cut a thin slice off the bottom of each shell so that it stands upright. Set aside while you prepare the soufflé mixture.

In a medium bowl, beat the egg yolks until very thick and light in color.

In another medium bowl, combine the egg whites with the lemon juice, and beat until firm but still glossy.

Stir the ham, mustard, pepper, and Tabasco into the yolks, then fold in the whites.

Spoon or pipe the mixture into the potato shells and bake for 5 to 10 minutes, or until the soufflés are puffy and browned on top.

NOTE: These soufflés can also be baked in individual molds. Butter the molds, spoon in the mixture, and bake in a preheated 400°F. oven for 8 to 10 minutes. Be sure to use smoked ham for this recipe; the smoky flavor is important to the success of the soufflé.

CAVIAR SOUFFLÉ

Nothing is more lush than caviar made into a soufflé. You can bake this soufflé either on top of toasted rounds of French bread, or in individual soufflé molds.

SERVES 6 AS AN APPETIZER
OR FIRST COURSE

- **12 thin rounds of day-old French bread, or 6 individual molds**
- **2 egg yolks**
- **3 egg whites**
- **1 teaspoon lemon juice**
- **Dash of Dijon mustard**
- **2 tablespoons black caviar, the best you can afford**

If using molds, butter the inside surfaces, including the rims, and refrigerate until ready to fill. If using French bread rounds, preheat the oven to 350° F., place rounds on a baking sheet, and toast for about 10 minutes, or until crisp and slightly browned.

Raise the oven temperature to 400° F.

To prepare the soufflé, beat the egg yolks in a medium bowl until very thick and light in color.

In another medium bowl, beat the whites with lemon juice until they are firm but still glossy.

Stir the mustard and the caviar into the yolks, then fold in the whites.

Spoon the mixture into prepared molds or onto the toasted rounds. Bake 8 to 10 minutes for soufflé molds and 5 to 7 minutes for toasted rounds, or until puffy and browned on top.

GOUGÈRES SOUFFLÉ WITH CHUNKY TOMATO SAUCE

Gougères are cream puffs that are flavored with cheese. Filled with this delicate Parmesan soufflé and served with fresh tomato sauce, they make an unusual, flavorful luncheon dish. The gougères can be prepared ahead and frozen, then brought to room temperature before baking.

SERVES 8 FOR LUNCH

GOUGÈRES

1 cup water

½ cup (1 stick) unsalted butter

1 ⅓ cups all-purpose flour

6 eggs

2 cups grated fontina cheese

SOUFFLÉ

3 egg yolks

5 egg whites

Few drops of lemon juice

½ teaspoon salt

1 teaspoon Dijon mustard

½ teaspoon dried oregano

¼ cup grated Parmesan cheese

TOMATO SAUCE

6 to 8 ripe tomatoes

1 tablespoon olive oil

Salt and pepper

Preheat the oven to 400° F.

To make the gougères, put the water and butter in a medium saucepan and set over medium-high heat. Adjust the heat so that the butter is melted about the same time the water begins to boil. Off the heat, add the flour all at once, and stir in well with a wooden spoon. Place saucepan back over medium heat, and stir constantly until the mixture forms a rubbery ball around the spoon and a film begins to form on the sides of the pan. This indicates that the flour is cooked.

Off the heat, add the eggs one at a time, beating with a wooden spoon or an electric mixer after each addition until well incorporated. Beat in the fontina cheese.

Spoon or pipe the batter onto a parchment-covered baking sheet, forming eight 3-inch rounded mounds about 2 inches apart. Bake for 20 minutes. Reduce the heat to 350° F. and bake 10 to 15 minutes more, until very brown and puffy. Let cool slightly, then cut a thin slice off the top of each and set aside until ready to fill.

Raise the oven temperature to 400° F.

While the gougères are cooling, prepare the soufflé batter. (If you do this sooner, the batter will lose volume by the time the gougères are ready to fill.) Beat the egg yolks in a large bowl until very thick and light in color.

In another large bowl, beat the whites with the lemon juice and salt until firm but still glossy. Stir the mustard, oregano, and Parmesan into the yolks, then fold in the whites.

To fill the gougères, first gently pull out any uncooked parts from the insides, being careful not to split the bottoms or sides. Spoon the soufflé mixture into the center of each. Replace tops. Bake for 8 to 10 minutes, or until the soufflés are puffy.

Meanwhile, peel and chop the tomatoes. Sauté in the olive oil, add salt and pepper to taste, and cook briefly; the tomatoes should stay chunky. Serve the sauce on the side.

MUSHROOM SOUFFLÉ IN VOL-AU-VENTS

Vol-au-vents are little cases of puff pastry. Filled with mushroom soufflé and served with a shallot-vermouth sauce, they make an elegant main course for lunch, or a fancy first course for an important dinner.

SERVES 6

VOL-AU-VENTS

1 (16-ounce) package frozen puff pastry (Saucier brand puff pastry works well here)

1 egg yolk

1 tablespoon heavy cream

SOUFFLÉ

1 tablespoon unsalted butter

1/3 cup finely chopped fresh mushrooms

3 egg yolks

4 egg whites

Few drops of lemon juice

1 tablespoon heavy cream

Dash of cayenne (ground red) pepper

1 **teaspoon salt**

½ **teaspoon white pepper**

SHALLOT-VERMOUTH SAUCE

1½ **teaspoons unsalted butter**

2 **tablespoons finely chopped shallots**

1 **clove garlic, crushed**

¾ **cup dry vermouth or dry white wine**

½ **cup heavy cream**

Pinch each of salt and black pepper

Preheat the oven to 400° F.

To make the *vol-au-vents*, roll out the pastry dough according to package directions to about a ¼-inch thickness. Using a 4-inch round biscuit cutter, cut out 6 circles and place them on an ungreased baking sheet. Center a 3-inch cutter over each circle of dough, and press down without quite cutting all the way through. The idea is to separate some layers of dough from the center so they can be lifted out after they're baked to form the top of the pastry case. Chill in refrigerator or freezer ½ hour.

Beat together the egg yolk and heavy cream just until well combined. Brush over the pastry circles, making sure none runs down the sides. (This would prevent the circles from rising properly.)

Bake for 10 minutes. Reduce the oven temperature to

350° F. and bake another 15 minutes, or until the *vol-au-vents* have risen and are well browned. Don't open the oven door until near the end of the baking time or the *vol-au-vents* may fall. Remove the tops from the *vol-au-vents* and let them cool, then carefully scoop out any uncooked layers of dough.

Raise the oven temperature to 400° F.

To make the soufflé, melt the butter in a small frying pan and add the mushrooms. Sauté for about 5 minutes, or until cooked through. Drain off any liquid that may have accumulated and reserve.

In a medium bowl, beat the egg yolks until very thick and light in color.

In another medium bowl, beat the egg whites with the lemon juice until stiff but still glossy. Stir the mushrooms, heavy cream, cayenne and salt and pepper into the yolks, then fold in the whites.

Fill the *vol-au-vents* with the mixture, replace the pastry tops, and bake for 8 to 10 minutes, or until the soufflé is puffy.

While the soufflés are baking, prepare the sauce. Melt the butter in a small frying pan and add the shallots and garlic. Sauté gently for about 5 minutes, until transparent and soft. Add the vermouth or wine and any reserved mushroom juices. Boil over high heat until the liquid is reduced by half. Add the cream and reduce again until you have a thick sauce. Add salt and pepper.

Pour a bit of sauce over each soufflé before serving.

VEGETABLE OMELETTE SOUFFLÉ

High in protein and low in fat, this is a dieter's dream.

*** SERVES 2 FOR LUNCH ***

½ **cup finely chopped leeks (white part only)**

½ **cup finely chopped red or green bell pepper**

½ **cup finely chopped zucchini**

2 **large, ripe tomatoes, finely chopped**

1 **clove garlic, peeled and minced**

  Salt and pepper

4 **egg yolks**

5 **egg whites**

  Few drops of lemon juice

Preheat the oven to 400° F.

Combine 1 teaspoon water with the leeks, pepper, zucchini, tomatoes, and garlic in a medium saucepan. Set over medium-high heat, cover, and cook about 15 minutes, until the vegetables are almost tender. Uncover and cook over high heat for about 5 minutes more, until almost dry. Add salt and pepper to taste.

In a large bowl, beat the egg yolks until very thick and light in color.

In another large bowl, beat the egg whites with the lemon juice until firm but still glossy. Fold the vegetables into the yolks, then fold in the whites.

Lightly coat an 8-inch nonstick ovenproof frying pan or omelette pan with vegetable oil and spoon in the soufflé mixture. Bake for about 15 minutes, or until puffy and browned on top.

CRAB SOUFFLÉ TARTS

These rich, elegant little soufflés are baked in shell-shaped pastry crusts, which are made by forming and baking the dough over the outside of scallop-shell baking dishes. These dishes, available in kitchenware shops and some department stores, are also useful for other seafood gratins, as well as for the Piña Colada Soufflé on page 58.

SERVES 6

½ **recipe Flaky Pastry Dough (page 100)**

3 **egg yolks**

4 **egg whites**

1 **teaspoon lemon juice**

1 **tablespoon mayonnaise**

2 **teaspoons Dijon mustard**

2 **teaspoons fresh dill, feathery parts only, chopped**

½ **teaspoon salt**

½ **teaspoon ground white pepper**

6 **ounces crab meat, well picked**

Preheat the oven to 350° F.

To prepare the shell crusts, roll the dough into a large round about ⅛ inch thick.

Using a very sharp knife, cut the dough into 6 pieces slightly larger than the baking dishes. Cover inverted dishes with the dough, pressing firmly. Trim away the edges of the pastry. Prick the pastry all over with a fork, and bake for about 15 minutes, or until well browned. Let pastries cool on the dishes, then separate.

Raise the oven temperature to 400° F. Meanwhile, prepare the soufflés.

In a medium bowl, beat the egg yolks until very thick and light in color.

In another medium bowl, beat the egg whites with the lemon juice until firm but still glossy. Stir the mayonnaise, mustard, dill, salt, pepper, and crab into the yolks, then fold in the whites.

Fill the pastry shells with the mixture and bake for about 8 minutes, or until puffy and browned on top.

VEGETABLE BOAT SOUFFLÉ

This savory chèvre soufflé is baked in a boat-shaped container fashioned from strips of colorful vegetable skins. It makes a lovely first course for a dinner for two.

SERVES 2

1 small zucchini

1 small yellow squash

1 small eggplant

1 tablespoon salt

2 egg yolks

Dash of Dijon mustard

1½ ounces chèvre (goat cheese)

¼ teaspoon chopped fresh dill

2 egg whites

1 teaspoon lemon juice

Using a vegetable peeler, remove the skins from the vegetables in long, thin strips about ¾ inch wide. Try to remove only the skin and no flesh. Put the eggplant strips in a colander and sprinkle with the salt. Let stand for 20 minutes. (This is to remove any bitterness in the eggplant.) Rinse under cold running water and dry well.

To make the forms for the boats you need four 6 × 6-inch pieces of aluminum foil. Fold each piece of foil into thirds. Press together the ends of 2 of the foil pieces to form them into an oval boat shape. Repeat with the other 2 pieces. Lay the boats on a buttered baking sheet; the sheet will form the bottom of the boats. Butter insides of the boats.

Starting at one end of a boat, lay the vegetable strips crosswise across the foil, pressing them gently against the sides and bottom. Overlap the strips and alternate colors. The strips will adhere to one another when they're baked.

Preheat the oven to 400° F.

To make the soufflés, beat the egg yolks with the mustard and chèvre in a small bowl until very thick and light in color. Stir in the dill.

In another small bowl, beat the egg whites with the lemon juice until firm but still glossy. Fold into the yolks.

Spoon the mixture into the prepared boats. Bake for 8 to 10 minutes, or until the soufflés are puffy and browned on top. Carefully remove the foil from the boats before serving.

CHICKEN LIVER SOUFFLÉ OMELETTE

W_e also enjoy this soufflé cold, the day after preparation.

SERVES 2 FOR LUNCH

- 1 **teaspoon unsalted butter**
- 4 **ounces chicken livers**
- 3 **tablespoons minced onion**
- 2 **egg yolks**
- 2 **slices bacon, cooked and crumbled**
  Vinaigrette made with 1 tablespoon tarragon vinegar, ¼ cup sesame oil, ½ teaspoon mustard, and salt and pepper
- 4 **egg whites**
  Few drops of lemon juice

Preheat the oven to 400° F.

Melt the butter in a small skillet and add the chicken livers and onion. Cook gently for 5 minutes, until the livers are just cooked through. Purée half the livers and coarsely chop the rest.

Beat the egg yolks in a medium bowl until thick and light in color. Stir in the liver purée and chopped livers, onion, bacon, and vinaigrette.

In another medium bowl, beat the egg whites with the lemon juice until they are firm but still glossy. Fold into the chicken-liver mixture.

Butter an 8-inch nonstick ovenproof skillet or omelette pan. Spoon the soufflé mixture into the pan and bake for 8 to 10 minutes, or until puffy and brown.

CARROT AND SQUASH SOUFFLÉ

If you have any leftover purée it can be reheated, mixed with a tablespoon or two of butter, and served as a delicious side dish at lunch or supper.

SERVES 6

1 **medium butternut squash (acorn squash can be substituted)**

2 **large carrots**

1 **teaspoon chopped fresh rosemary**

1 **tablespoon minced shallots**

1 **teaspoon butter**

3 **egg yolks**

¾ **teaspoon salt**

½ **teaspoon pepper**

5 **egg whites**

1 **teaspoon lime juice**

Preheat oven to 400° F. Butter 6 individual soufflé molds or one 8-cup mold.

Place whole, unpeeled squash in a shallow baking

dish and bake for 30 to 45 minutes or until tender. Discard seeds, remove pulp, and measure out ½ cup. Set aside. Remove tops from carrots, scrape clean, and cut into 1-inch slices. Cook in boiling water to cover until tender. Drain. Measure out ½ cup. Purée the squash, carrots, and rosemary together in a blender or food processor.

Sauté the shallots in the butter until softened. In a medium bowl, beat the egg yolks until very thick and light in color. Fold in the vegetable purée, shallots, salt and pepper.

In another medium bowl, beat the egg whites with the lime juice and a dash of salt until they hold soft peaks. Fold the whites into the vegetable mixture. Spoon or pipe into prepared mold or molds.

Bake 8 to 10 minutes for individual molds, 15 to 18 minutes for the larger mold, or until puffy. Because of its substantial vegetable content, this soufflé will not puff quite as high as the others, but its intense flavor is compensation.

BAKED

SWEET

SOUFFLÉS

ORANGE SOUFFLÉ

The orange essence used here, which is derived from the zest (the orange-colored part of the peel), makes a versatile flavoring that can be used in various sauces and buttercreams. This dessert soufflé is light in texture but very intensely orange in flavor.

SERVES 2

2 large, bright-skinned navel oranges

1 egg yolk

4 teaspoons sugar

1 teaspoon lemon juice

2 egg whites

Preheat the oven to 400° F. Butter and sugar 2 individual soufflé molds. Refrigerate until ready to fill.

To make the orange essence, finely grate the skin of 1 orange, making sure you remove only the orange part. Juice both oranges. Set aside about one-quarter of the juice, and put the rest in a small saucepan with the grated zest. Boil over medium-high heat, watching it carefully, until reduced to about 2 tablespoons. It should be very thick and syrupy. Remove from heat, let cool, then add the reserved juice.

In a small bowl, beat the egg yolk with 2 teaspoons of the sugar and the lemon juice until very thick and light in color.

In another small bowl, beat the whites until foamy. Gradually add the remaining 2 teaspoons sugar while continuing to beat until firm but still glossy. Stir the orange essence into the yolks, then fold in the whites. Spoon or pipe the mixture into the prepared molds and bake for 8 to 10 minutes, or until puffy and browned on top.

CHESTNUT SOUFFLÉ WITH CRANBERRY COULIS

The combination of sweet and tart flavors makes this soufflé a perfect finale for Thanksgiving or Christmas dinner.

SERVES 2

3 tablespoons chestnut purée

3½ tablespoons chestnut spread (sweetened puréed chestnuts; we prefer Clément Faugier brand)

1 egg yolk

2 egg whites

Few drops of lemon juice

1 tablespoon sugar

1 tablespoon dark rum

Cranberry Coulis (recipe follows)

Preheat the oven to 400° F. Butter and sugar 2 individual soufflé molds, and refrigerate until ready to fill.

Combine the chestnut purée and the chestnut spread in a small bowl. Beat with a wooden spoon or electric mixer until smooth. Add the egg yolk and beat again until smooth.

In another small bowl, beat the egg whites with the lemon juice until foamy. Add the sugar gradually while continuing to beat until the whites are firm but still glossy.

Stir the rum into the yolks, then fold in the whites.

Spoon or pipe the mixture into the prepared molds. Bake for 8 to 10 minutes, or until the soufflés are puffy and browned on top.

Serve with the Cranberry Coulis passed separately so each diner can spoon a bit into the center of his or her soufflé.

NOTE: Both the chestnut spread and purée are available at specialty shops and some supermarkets.

CRANBERRY COULIS

MAKES 2 CUPS

1 cup fresh or frozen and thawed cranberries

1 cup cranberry juice

Sugar to taste (the mixture should be tart)

Rinse the cranberries under cold running water and pick over carefully. Place all the ingredients in a blender (preferably) or food processor, and purée until smooth.

The sauce can be made several days ahead and kept covered and refrigerated. Bring to room temperature before serving.

CHEESECAKE SOUFFLÉ

This soufflé has the satisfying flavor, but not the heaviness, of cheesecake.

SERVES 6

4 egg yolks

4 tablespoons sugar

6 egg whites

Few drops of lemon juice

2 teaspoons grated lime zest

1 teaspoon vanilla extract

6 ounces cream cheese, at room temperature

Preheat the oven to 400° F. Butter and sugar 6 individual soufflé molds. Refrigerate until ready to fill.

In a large bowl, beat the egg yolks with 2 tablespoons of the sugar until very thick and light in color.

In a medium bowl, beat the egg whites with the lemon juice until foamy. Gradually add the remaining sugar while continuing to beat until firm but still glossy.

Beat the lime zest, vanilla, and cream cheese into the egg yolks, then fold in the egg whites.

Spoon or pipe the mixture into the prepared molds and bake for 8 to 10 minutes, or until puffy and browned on top.

YOGURT SOUFFLÉ

Here is a rich-tasting but relatively low-fat dessert to add to your repertoire.

SERVES 3

- ½ **cup low-fat small-curd cottage cheese**
- ½ **cup plain low-fat yogurt**
- 2 **tablespoons unsweetened raspberry or blackberry jam**
- 1 **tablespoon maple syrup**
- 2 **egg whites**

  Few drops of lemon juice
- 1 **tablespoon sugar**

Preheat the oven to 350° F. Butter and sugar 3 individual soufflé molds, and refrigerate until ready to fill.

Using a fork, blender, or food processor, combine the cottage cheese with 1 tablespoon of the yogurt until smooth. Place in a medium bowl and beat in the remaining yogurt, jam, and maple syrup until smooth.

In a small bowl, beat the egg whites with the lemon juice until foamy, then gradually add the sugar while continuing to beat until the whites are firm but still glossy. Fold into the yogurt mixture.

Spoon or pipe the batter into the molds and bake for 15 to 20 minutes, or until puffy and browned on top.

SPICY PUMPKIN SOUFFLÉ WITH COMPOTE OF ORANGES

The compote of oranges, with its hint of Middle Eastern spicing, complements this pumpkin soufflé, but the soufflé can also stand very nicely on its own.

SERVES 5

COMPOTE OF ORANGES

5 large navel oranges

Grated zest of 1 lime

1 teaspoon ground cinnamon

½ teaspoon ground cardamom

¼ teaspoon ground cumin

SOUFFLÉ

3 egg yolks

5 tablespoons sugar

5 egg whites

Few drops of lemon juice

2 tablespoons skim milk

1 teaspoon ground cinnamon

½ teaspoon ground ginger

¼ teaspoon ground allspice

½ teaspoon ground cloves

5 tablespoons canned, unsweetened pumpkin

To make the compote, peel the oranges and cut away any remaining white pith. Slice oranges crosswise.

Sprinkle the slices with the lime zest and spices, and combine well.

Store compote at room temperature until ready to serve.

Preheat the oven to 400° F. Butter and sugar 5 individual soufflé molds. Refrigerate until ready to fill.

In a large bowl, beat the egg yolks with 3 tablespoons of the sugar until very thick and light in color.

In a medium bowl, beat the egg whites with the lemon juice until foamy. Gradually add 1 tablespoon of sugar, continuing to beat until the whites are firm but still glossy.

Beat the milk, spices, and pumpkin into the yolks, then fold in the whites.

Spoon or pipe the mixture into the prepared molds, and sprinkle the tops with the remaining tablespoon of sugar. Bake for 8 to 10 minutes, or until puffy and browned on top.

Serve immediately, placing each mold on an individual plate. Pass the compote separately.

RUM RAISIN SOUFFLÉ
WITH CARAMEL SAUCE

The caramel sauce can be made a day or two ahead. You'll have a little more than 1 cup left over; use it to top ice cream or fresh fruit.

SERVES 4

CARAMEL SAUCE

1 cup sugar

½ cup water

1 cup heavy cream

SOUFFLÉ

⅔ cup raisins

2 tablespoons dark rum

2 egg yolks

2 tablespoons sugar

4 egg whites

Few drops of lemon juice

Combine the raisins and rum, and put aside to soak for 1 hour, if possible, before you make the soufflés. Prepare the caramel sauce. Have ready a pastry brush, a long-handled wire whisk, and an oven mitt. Combine the sugar and water in a small saucepan, either heavy aluminum, stainless steel, enameled cast-iron, or copper. Place over medium heat and bring to a boil. As the sugar is heating, dip a pastry brush in cold water and run it around the inside of the saucepan just above the level of the sugar. This will wash away any sugar crystals clinging to the sides of the pan; these crystals can multiply and prevent the sugar from melting smoothly.

As the sugar boils, move the pot gently back and forth over the burner to ensure even heat distribution. The sugar will turn golden, then nut-colored. When it smells like caramel and gives off little wisps of smoke, immediately remove from the heat. The caramel will burn very quickly at this point.

Put on the oven mitt, stand back a bit, and add the heavy cream very slowly, stirring rapidly as you pour. The sugar will bubble up and may spatter, but it will calm down as it cools. Set the sauce aside.

Preheat the oven to 400° F. Butter and sugar 4 individual soufflé molds, and refrigerate until ready to fill.

Prepare the soufflés. In a medium bowl, beat the egg yolks with 1 tablespoon of the sugar until very thick and light in color.

In another medium bowl, beat the whites with the lemon juice until foamy. Gradually add the remaining sugar while continuing to beat until the whites are firm but still glossy.

Stir ¼ cup of the Caramel Sauce and the raisins into the yolks, then fold in the whites. Spoon into the molds and bake for 8 to 10 minutes, or until puffy and browned on top.

HOT BERRY SOUFFLÉ

This makes a wonderful finish for a summertime dinner party. The sliced peaches are a good foil for the raspberries.

SERVES 6

SOUFFLÉ

- **1 pint fresh raspberries (approximately ½ pound)**
- **3 egg yolks**
- **4 egg whites**
- **⅓ cup sugar**
- **2 ripe peaches, peeled and sliced**
- **Raspberry Coulis (page 113)**

Preheat the oven to 375° F. Butter and sugar 6 individual soufflé molds, and refrigerate until ready to fill.

Puree the raspberries in a blender or food processor, then press through a sieve to remove tiny seeds.

In a large bowl, beat the egg yolks until very thick and light in color.

In another large bowl, beat the egg whites until foamy, then add the sugar gradually while continuing to beat until whites are firm but still glossy.

Stir the berry purée into the yolks, then fold in the

whites. Spoon the mixture into the mold and bake for 8 to 10 minutes, or until puffy and browned on top.

Serve with the sliced peaches on the side and a spoonful of Raspberry Coulis on top.

SURPRISE SOUFFLÉ

Hidden inside each seemingly innocent little chocolate soufflé is an intensely flavored orange soufflé.

SERVES 6

2 **large, bright-skinned navel oranges**

4 **egg yolks**

3 **tablespoons sugar**

6 **egg whites**

Few drops of lemon juice

Grated zest of 1 large orange

2 **tablespoons Grand Marnier**

2 **tablespoons unsweetened cocoa powder**

Finely grate the skin of the oranges, making sure to use only the orange zest. Juice the oranges. Set aside about one-quarter of the juice, and put the rest in a small saucepan with half the grated zest. Boil over medium-high heat, watching it carefully, until reduced to about 2 tablespoons. The mixture should be very thick and syrupy. Remove from heat, let cool, then add the reserved juice.

Preheat the oven to 400° F. Have ready 2 pastry bags, both fitted with a ¼-inch plain tip. Butter and sugar 6 individual soufflé molds, and refrigerate until ready to fill.

In a large bowl, beat the egg yolks with 2 tablespoons of the sugar until very thick and light in color.

In another large bowl, combine the egg whites with the lemon juice, and beat until foamy. Gradually add the remaining sugar while continuing to beat until the whites are firm but still glossy. Fold into the yolks.

Spoon about one-third of the mixture into another mixing bowl. Add the reduced orange syrup, the remaining grated zest, and Grand Marnier. Fold until blended. To the remaining portion of the mixture add the cocoa, and fold until blended.

Fill 1 pastry bag with the orange mixture, the other with the chocolate. Pipe the chocolate batter around the sides of the molds, leaving the centers empty. Make sure to pipe the batter all the way to the tops of the molds, and leave some chocolate mixture in the bag to pipe over the tops later.

Quickly pipe the orange mixture into the centers of the molds, stopping about halfway from the top. Pipe a layer of chocolate all across the top of each, and smooth it carefully with a spatula so that the orange is completely hidden. Bake for 8 to 10 minutes, or until puffy and browned on top.

GREEN APPLE SOUFFLÉ
WITH CINNAMON

Like apple pie but not the crust? This soufflé will surprise you. Calvados Sauce — Crème Anglaise doused with apple brandy — adds richness.

SERVES 6

- **2 egg yolks**
- **2 tablespoons sugar**
- **3 egg whites**
- **Few drops of lemon juice**
- **1 tablespoon apricot preserves**
- **½ teaspoon ground cinnamon**
- **2 large Granny Smith apples, peeled and chopped fine**
- **Calvados Sauce (page 112)**

Preheat the oven to 400° F. Butter and sugar 6 individual soufflé molds, and refrigerate until ready to fill.

In a medium bowl, beat egg yolks with 1 tablespoon of the sugar until very thick and light in color.

In another medium bowl, beat the egg whites with the lemon juice until foamy. Gradually add the remaining tablespoon of sugar while continuing to beat until whites are firm but still glossy.

Stir the apricot preserves, cinnamon, and apples into the yolks, then fold in the whites. Spoon or pipe into molds.

Bake for 8 to 10 minutes, or until puffy and browned on top. Serve with Calvados Sauce, if desired.

APRICOT SOUFFLÉ WITH WHITE-WINE SABAYON

A white-wine sabayon makes this soufflé one of the most elegant desserts you could serve to guests. Apricots provide an unusual and slightly mysterious flavor.

SERVES 4

SOUFFLÉ

- ½ **cup (4 ounces) canned apricots, packed in sugar-free juice, drained**
- 2 **egg yolks**
- 2 **tablespoons sugar**
- 4 **egg whites**

  Few drops of lemon juice
- 2 **tablespoons apricot preserves**

  Grated zest of 1 large orange
- 1 **tablespoon Grand Marnier**

WHITE-WINE SABAYON

- ½ **cup white wine**
- ¼ **cup sugar**
- 3 **egg yolks**

Preheat the oven to 400° F. Butter and sugar 4 individual soufflé molds, and refrigerate until ready to fill.

Purée the apricots in a blender or food processor. Set aside.

In a medium bowl, beat the egg yolks with 1 tablespoon of the sugar until very thick and light in color.

In another medium bowl, beat the egg whites with the lemon juice until foamy, then add the remaining tablespoon sugar while continuing to beat until whites are firm but still glossy.

Stir the apricot purée, apricot preserves, orange zest, and Grand Marnier into the yolks, then fold in the whites.

Spoon or pipe the mixture into the prepared molds and bake for 8 to 10 minutes, or until puffy and browned on top.

While the soufflés are baking, prepare the sabayon. In a small saucepan or sabayon pan, whip together the wine, sugar, and egg yolks. Holding the pan near but not directly over medium-high heat, whip the mixture constantly until it is very thick and foamy.

Serve the sauce immediately, passing it separately so that diners can spoon a little into the middle of their soufflés.

HALF-AND-HALF
MOCHA-ORANGE
SOUFFLÉ

Here is a "surprise" soufflé with a heavenly combination of flavors.

SERVES 8

2 large, bright-skinned navel oranges

2 tablespoons instant espresso powder

1 tablespoon dark rum

4 egg yolks

4 tablespoons sugar

8 egg whites

Few drops of lemon juice

Finely grate the skin of 1 orange, making sure to use only the orange zest. Juice both oranges. Set aside about one-quarter of the juice, and put the rest in a small saucepan with the grated zest. Boil over medium-high heat, watching it carefully, until reduced to about 2 tablespoons. The mixture should be very thick and syrupy. Remove from heat, let cool, then add the reserved juice.

Preheat the oven to 400° F. Butter and sugar 8 individual soufflé molds, and refrigerate until ready to fill.

In a small bowl, dissolve the espresso powder in the rum. Set aside.

In a large bowl, whip the egg yolks with 3 tablespoons of the sugar until very thick and light in color.

In another large bowl, beat the egg whites with the lemon juice until foamy. Add the remaining sugar gradually while continuing to beat until whites are firm but still glossy. Fold into the yolks.

Place about half the mixture in a separate bowl, and fold in the espresso-rum mixture. Fold 2 tablespoons of the orange syrup into the remaining half. (You'll have about 1 tablespoon of orange syrup left over; it can be kept, covered and refrigerated, for a day or so and used to flavor cakes, custards, pancakes, or muffins.)

Using 2 pastry bags, each fitted with ¼-inch plain tips, pipe the orange batter into each soufflé mold, then top the orange batter with the mocha batter. Bake for 8 to 10 minutes, or until puffy and browned on top.

PIÑA COLADA SOUFFLÉ

You can add to the tropical feeling of this soufflé by baking and serving it in a scallop-shell baking dish sold in kitchenware stores.

SERVES 2

½ cup ½-inch cubes homemade Sponge Cake (page 104) or store-bought ladyfingers

2 tablespoons dark rum

2 tablespoons finely chopped fresh pineapple or canned (in sugar-free juice), with juice

1 egg yolk

2½ tablespoons sweetened, grated coconut

2 egg whites

Few drops of lemon juice

2 tablespoons sugar

Preheat the oven to 400° F.

Butter and sugar 2 shell baking dishes or soufflé molds, and refrigerate until ready to fill.

Pour the rum over the cake cubes and let them soak for 5 minutes.

If using fresh pineapple, place it in a clean dish towel and squeeze dry over a bowl. Save 1 tablespoon of the juice. If using canned pineapple, drain it well but save 1 tablespoon of the juice.

In a small bowl, beat the egg yolk with the pineapple juice until very thick and light in color. Add the cake cubes, chopped pineapple, and coconut.

In another small bowl, beat the egg whites with the lemon juice until foamy. Gradually add the sugar while continuing to beat until whites are firm but still glossy. Fold into the yolk-pineapple mixture.

Spoon into prepared shells or molds, and bake for 8 to 10 minutes, or until puffy and browned on top.

BROWNIE SOUFFLÉ WITH WHIPPED CREAM

This rich confection is a must for chocolate lovers.

SERVES 6

3 tablespoons Pastry Cream (page 99)

4 ounces good-quality bittersweet chocolate, melted

3 tablespoons unsweetened cocoa powder

3 egg whites

Few drops of lemon juice

3 tablespoons granulated sugar

3 egg yolks

WHIPPED CREAM

1 cup heavy cream

1 tablespoon confectioners' sugar

2 tablespoons dark rum

Preheat the oven to 400° F. Butter and sugar 6 individual soufflé molds, and refrigerate until ready to fill.

In a medium bowl, stir together the pastry cream, melted chocolate, and cocoa.

In another medium bowl, beat the egg whites with the lemon juice until foamy. Gradually add the sugar while continuing to beat until whites are firm but still glossy.

Beat the egg yolks into the chocolate mixture, then gently stir in about one-quarter of the egg whites to lighten the mixture. Fold in the remaining egg whites.

Spoon into the prepared molds and bake for 8 to 10 minutes, or until puffy and browned on top.

Meanwhile, whip the cream with the confectioners' sugar and rum until it holds soft peaks. Serve the soufflés as soon as they come out of the oven. Pass the whipped cream separately.

PANCAKE GÂTEAU WITH FRANGELICO AND HAZELNUTS

Ground hazelnuts (filberts) are available in specialty stores and sometimes health food stores as well.

SERVES 6

- **⅔ cup ½-inch cubes homemade Sponge Cake (page 104) or store-bought ladyfingers**
- **¼ cup Frangelico (hazelnut liqueur)**
- **2 egg yolks**
- **4 tablespoons sugar**
- **3 egg whites**
- **Few drops of lemon juice**
- **¼ cup ground hazelnuts**
- **18 (3-inch) Crêpes or 6 (7-inch) Crêpes (page 106)**

Preheat the oven to 400° F.

Butter and sugar 6 individual soufflé molds or one 6-cup mold, and refrigerate until ready to fill.

Pour the Frangelico over the cake cubes, toss, and let the cubes soak for 5 minutes. In a medium bowl, beat the egg yolks with 2 tablespoons of the sugar until very thick and light in color.

In another medium bowl, beat the egg whites with the lemon juice until foamy. Gradually add the remaining sugar while continuing to beat until the whites are firm but still glossy.

Fold the cake cubes and ground hazelnuts into the yolks, then fold in the whites.

Alternate layers of crêpes and soufflé batter in the soufflé mold(s), beginning with crêpes and ending with batter. Bake for 8 to 10 minutes for individual soufflés and about 20 minutes for the large size, or until puffy and browned on top.

OMELETTE SOUFFLÉ
WITH BANANAS AND
RUM

Bananas and rum give this soufflé a Jamaican quality.

SERVES 6

2 medium or 3 small, ripe bananas

4½ tablespoons sugar

2 tablespoons (¼ stick) unsalted butter

3 tablespoons dark rum

1 tablespoon plus a few drops of lemon juice

3 egg yolks

4 egg whites

Preheat the oven to 400° F.

Slice the bananas into ½-inch-thick pieces and toss with 1 tablespoon of the sugar.

Set an 8-inch ovenproof omelette pan or frying pan over high heat and add the butter. When the butter is sizzling hot, add the bananas. Sprinkle over 1 tablespoon of the rum and the tablespoon of lemon juice, and toss the bananas quickly over high heat to caramelize. Remove from heat, leaving bananas in the pan.

In a medium bowl, beat the egg yolks with 2 tablespoons of the sugar until very thick and light in color.

In another medium bowl, beat the egg whites with the few drops of lemon juice and ½ tablespoon of the sugar until the whites are firm but still glossy. Fold the rum into the yolks, then fold in the whites.

Cover the bananas with the soufflé mixture and smooth the top. Sprinkle over the remaining tablespoon of sugar. Bake for 8 to 10 minutes, or until puffy and browned on top.

STRIPED LIME-COCOA SOUFFLÉ

The flavors of chocolate and lime were made for each other, and as you'll see when you spoon into this tasty soufflé, the color combination is striking as well.

SERVES 2

1 egg yolk

3 tablespoons sugar

2 egg whites

Few drops of lemon juice

Juice from 1½ small limes

1 tablespoon unsweetened cocoa powder

Preheat the oven to 400° F.

Have ready 2 pastry bags, each fitted with a ¼-inch plain tip. Butter and sugar 2 individual soufflé molds, and refrigerate until ready to fill.

In a small bowl, beat the egg yolk with 2 tablespoons of the sugar until very thick and light in color.

In another small bowl, beat the egg whites with the lemon juice until foamy. Gradually add the remaining sugar while continuing to beat until whites are firm but still glossy. Stir the lime juice into the yolks, then fold in the whites.

Place one-quarter of the mixture in a separate small bowl and add the cocoa, folding it in thoroughly.

Put the cocoa mixture in one pastry bag, the plain mixture in the other. Pipe straight bottom-to-top lines of cocoa mixture around the sides of the molds, spacing them ¼ to ½ inch apart. Pipe plain batter between the lines of chocolate and then into the center of the molds, filling them nearly to the top.

Bake for 8 to 10 minutes, or until puffy and browned on top.

LEMON TART SOUFFLÉ

Here's a light, triple-layer soufflé-type twist on lemon meringue pie.

SERVES 8

- **8 baked 3- or 4-inch tartlet shells, made from Flaky Pastry Dough (page 100)**
- **4 medium lemons, preferably thin skinned**
- **4 eggs**
- **½ cup plus 2 tablespoons sugar**
- **2 egg whites**

Preheat the oven to 375° F. Have the tartlet shells ready.

Grate the skins of the lemons, making sure to remove only the bright yellow zest. Juice the lemons. In a large bowl, mix the eggs, lemon zest, all but a few drops of the lemon juice, and ½ cup of the sugar. Whisk until smooth.

Fill a skillet or roasting pan large enough to hold the bowl with about 1 inch of water. Bring the water to a simmer. Place the mixing bowl in the pan and whisk the lemon cream over medium-low heat until it becomes very thick, about 10 minutes. Don't let it come to the boil or it will curdle. Remove from the heat, strain, and cool at room temperature.

When the lemon cream has cooled, whip the egg

whites with the few drops of lemon juice until foamy. Gradually add the remaining 2 tablespoons of sugar while continuing to beat until the whites are firm and very glossy.

Fold half the lemon cream into half the meringue. Fill the tart shells with a layer of plain lemon cream, then a layer of the meringue-lemon cream. Finish with a layer of plain meringue.

Bake for about 3 minutes, or until the meringue is browned.

ST. PATRICK'S DAY SOUFFLÉ

Green, then more green. But it would be a shame to restrict these soufflés just to St. Patrick's Day.

SERVES 2

⅔ cup ½-inch cubes homemade Sponge Cake (page 104) or store-bought ladyfingers

1½ tablespoons green Chartreuse liqueur

1½ tablespoons green Crème de Menthe

1 egg yolk

3 tablespoons sugar

2 egg whites

Few drops of lemon juice

Preheat the oven to 400° F.

Butter and sugar 2 individual soufflé molds, and refrigerate until ready to fill.

In separate bowls, soak half the cake cubes in Chartreuse and half in Crème de Menthe for 5 minutes.

In a small bowl, beat the egg yolk with half the sugar until very thick and light in color.

In another small bowl, beat the egg whites with the lemon juice until foamy, then gradually add the remaining sugar while continuing to beat until whites are firm but still glossy. Fold the whites into the yolk.

Divide the soufflé mixture in half. Into one half, fold the Chartreuse–soaked cake cubes; into the other half, the Crème de Menthe–soaked cubes.

Spoon one mixture into the bottom of the soufflé molds, then spoon the other mixture on top. Bake for 8 to 10 minutes, or until puffy and browned on top.

MAPLE SOUFFLÉ IN CRÊPES

The crêpes can be made early in the day, or even a day ahead and kept wrapped and refrigerated until ready to use.

SERVES 6

6 (7-inch) Crêpes (page 106)

2 egg yolks

2 tablespoons sugar

3 egg whites

Few drops of lemon juice

1 tablespoon maple syrup

1½ teaspoons maple extract

Preheat the oven to 400° F.

Butter a gratin dish just large enough to hold the folded crêpes in one layer.

In a medium bowl, beat the egg yolks with 1 tablespoon of the sugar until very thick and light in color.

In another medium bowl, beat the egg whites with the lemon juice until foamy, then add the remaining sugar gradually while continuing to beat until whites are firm but still glossy. Stir the maple syrup and extract into the yolks, then fold in the whites.

Place a crêpe in the gratin dish. Spoon a scant ½ cup of the soufflé mixture onto half of each crêpe. Fold the crêpe over the mixture to form a turnover shape. Continue to fill and fold the crêpes in the gratin dish, since they are difficult to move once they've been filled.

Bake for 8 to 10 minutes, or until the crêpes are puffy and browned on top. Serve with Mocha Sauce (page 112).

PEAR TARTLET SOUFFLÉ

Canned pears seem to be the most reliable in flavor, except in the fall, when you can substitute fresh pears cut in cubes and simmered in their own juices until soft.

SERVES 6

- **6 baked 3- or 4-inch tartlet shells made from Sweet Pastry Dough (page 102)**
- **½ cup ½-inch cubes homemade Sponge Cake (page 104) or store-bought ladyfingers**
- **2 tablespoons Pear William (*eau-de-vie de poire*)**
- **1 (10-ounce) can pears, packed in unsweetened juice**
- **1 egg yolk**
- **2 tablespoons sugar**
- **2 egg whites**
- **1 tablespoon lemon juice**

Preheat the oven to 400° F. Have the tartlet shells ready.

Put the cake cubes in a small bowl and sprinkle with the Poire William.

Drain the pears well and purée in an electric blender

or food processor. Remove to a medium bowl.

In a small bowl, beat the egg yolk with 1 tablespoon of the sugar until very thick and light in color.

In another small bowl, beat the egg whites with the lemon juice until foamy. Add the remaining sugar gradually while continuing to beat until whites are firm but still glossy.

Fold the yolk into the pear purée, then fold in the cake cubes. Fold in the whites. Fill the tartlet shells with the mixture and bake for 8 to 10 minutes, or until puffy and browned on top.

MONTE CARLO SOUFFLÉ

Two flavors of soufflé batter alternate on top of a cookie. These may seem tricky to prepare but they aren't.

SERVES 8

1 recipe Flaky Pastry Dough (page 100)

2 egg yolks

4 tablespoons sugar

4 egg whites

1½ tablespoons plus a few drops of lemon juice

Grated zest of 1 large lemon

⅓ cup fresh blueberries, strawberries, or raspberries, puréed in a blender or food processor to make 2 tablespoons purée

Preheat the oven to 350° F. Have ready 2 pastry bags with ¼-inch plain tips.

To prepare the cookies, roll the dough out to a ⅛-inch thickness. Cut out circles with a 4- or 5-inch biscuit cutter, and remove them carefully to a parchment-covered baking sheet, placing them 1 inch apart. You should have 8 circles.

Bake for about 10 minutes, or until lightly browned and cooked through. Remove to a baking rack and let cool while you prepare the soufflé mixture.

In a medium bowl, beat the egg yolks with half the sugar until very thick and light in color.

In another medium bowl, beat the egg whites and drops of lemon juice until foamy, then gradually add the rest of the sugar, continuing to beat until whites are firm but still glossy. Stir the 1½ tablespoons lemon juice and zest into the yolks, then fold in the whites.

Put half the soufflé mixture in a separate bowl and fold in the berry purée.

To form the cookie-soufflés, lay the cookies on a parchment-lined baking sheet. Pipe or spoon one flavor of batter onto the cookies, then carefully pipe or spoon the other flavor on top.

Bake for 8 to 10 minutes, or until puffy and browned on top.

TOASTED-COCONUT PECAN-PIE SOUFFLÉ

Lighter than traditional pecan pie but intense in flavor, the idea for this soufflé comes from the former Big Cheese restaurant in Washington, D.C. One taste and you may never go conventional again!

SERVES 6

6 baked 3- or 4-inch tartlet shells, made from Sweet Pastry Dough (page 102)

2 egg yolks

2 tablespoons sugar

3 egg whites

2 tablespoons plus a few drops of lemon juice

¼ cup chopped pecans

¼ cup shredded or grated coconut, toasted for 8 to 10 minutes in a 400° F. oven

1 teaspoon vanilla extract

Preheat the oven to 400° F. Have the tartlet shells ready.

In a medium bowl, beat the egg yolks with 1 tablespoon of the sugar until very thick and light in color.

In another medium bowl, beat the egg whites with the few drops of lemon juice until foamy. Add the remaining sugar gradually while continuing to beat until whites are firm but still glossy. Stir the pecans, coconut, 2 tablespoons of lemon juice, and vanilla into the yolks, then fold in the whites.

Spoon the mixture into the tartlet shells and bake for 8 to 10 minutes, or until puffy and browned on top.

TARTLET AMANDINE SOUFFLÉ

Duruing our tenure at Jean Louis at the Watergate restaurant, these tartlets had a faithful following. Rewardingly rich, these pastry-based soufflés will end a romantic dinner for two with a flourish.

SERVES 2

2 baked 3- to 4-inch tartlet shells, made from Flaky Pastry Dough (page 100)

1 egg yolk

2 egg whites

Few drops of lemon juice

1 tablespoon sugar

1 tablespoon almond paste

1 tablespoon ground almonds

1 tablespoon Amaretto (almond liqueur)

Preheat the oven to 400° F. Have tartlet shells ready. In a small bowl, beat the egg yolk until very thick and light in color.

In another small bowl, beat the egg whites with the lemon juice until foamy, then add the sugar while continuing to beat until firm but still glossy. Fold the almond paste, ground almonds, and Amaretto into the yolk, then fold in the whites.

Spoon the mixture into the tartlet shells and bake for 8 to 10 minutes, or until puffy and browned on top.

FROZEN

SOUFFLÉS

NOUGAT GLACÉ WITH RASPBERRY COULIS

A summertime dessert non-pareil. It's a bit involved to prepare but well worth the effort.

2 cups chopped glacéed fruits, such as cherries and pineapple

¾ cup dark rum

¼ cup water

½ cup sugar

4 egg whites

1 cup heavy cream

1 recipe Nougatine (page 114)

1 recipe Raspberry Coulis (page 113)

Macerate fruit in the rum overnight.

In a small saucepan, combine the water and sugar, and bring to a boil over medium-high heat. As the sugar syrup boils, agitate the pan gently but don't stir. Cook the syrup until it reaches the soft-ball stage, 238° F. on a candy thermometer.

As the sugar syrup approaches the required temperature, begin beating the egg whites, preferably with a stand-type electric mixer. When the sugar syrup is done, immediately pour it very slowly into the egg whites, beating constantly. Beat until the mixture is completely cooled, at least 5 minutes.

Whip the cream to fairly stiff peaks and fold it into the meringue, then fold in the Nougatine and the glacéed fruits. Line two 6-cup terrines or loaf pans with a layer of plastic wrap, then spoon in the mixture. Cover and freeze overnight. To unmold, turn upside down on a platter and the glacé will release. Peel off the plastic wrap, and slice the glacé.

To serve, pour a pool of Raspberry Coulis into chilled dessert plates. Place slices of glacé, one per plate, on top of the coulis.

GRAND MARNIER
SOUFFLÉ NEGRESCO

This is the basic frozen souf-
flé recipe used a few years ago at the Chanticleer Restaurant in the Negresco Hotel in Nice, France.

SERVES 6 TO 8

6 egg yolks

⅓ cup sugar

1 cup heavy cream

3 egg whites

Few drops of lemon juice

⅓ cup Grand Marnier

In a large bowl, combine the egg yolks and half the
sugar; beat until very thick and light in color.

In a medium bowl, whip the cream until it holds soft
peaks. Set aside.

In another medium bowl, beat the egg whites with the
lemon juice until foamy. Gradually add the remaining
sugar while continuing to beat until firm but still glossy.

Stir the Grand Marnier into the egg yolks. Gently fold
in the whipped cream, then fold in the egg whites.

Spoon the mixture into 8 individual soufflé molds,
leveling off the tops. For higher soufflés to serve 6, make

collars by folding sheets of aluminum foil into strips and wrapping the strips once around the molds. The upper edges of the strips should be about 1 inch above the tops of the molds. Secure with string. Fill molds to top of collar. Cover with plastic wrap, and freeze.

Serve either in the molds, with the foil collar removed, or unmolded onto chilled dessert plates.

CRANBERRY SOUFFLÉ GLACÉ WITH LIME SHERBET AND CRANBERRY PURÉE

Here is a variation on cranberries that makes a perfect dessert for Thanksgiving dinner. The recipe can be made several days ahead and can also be easily cut in half.

SERVES 10 TO 12

CRANBERRY PURÉE

1 (12-ounce) bag fresh cranberries

½ cup sugar

¼ cup water

½ cup cranberry juice cocktail

SOUFFLÉ

4 egg yolks

½ cup sugar

1 cup heavy cream

4 egg whites

2 tablespoons plus a few drops of lemon juice

2 tablespoons cassis (black currant liqueur)

1 pint good-quality lime sherbet, slightly softened

Prepare an 8-cup soufflé mold or 10 ¾-cup molds or 12 ⅔-cup individual soufflé molds. Make a standing foil collar for each mold by folding a sheet of aluminum foil into a strip and wrapping the strip once around the mold. The upper edge of the strip should be about 1 inch above the upper edge of the mold. Secure with string.

To prepare the cranberry purée, rinse the cranberries under cold running water and pick over carefully. Combine in a saucepan with the sugar and water. Bring to a boil over medium heat and boil just until the cranberries have popped. Let cool to room temperature, then purée in a blender or food processor. You'll need 2 cups of purée.

To make the soufflé, combine egg yolks and 6 tablespoons of the sugar in a large bowl. Beat until very thick and light in color.

In a medium bowl, whip the cream until soft peaks form. Set aside.

In another medium bowl, beat the egg whites with the few drops of lemon juice until foamy. Gradually add the remaining 2 tablespoons of sugar while continuing to beat until firm but still glossy.

Stir 1½ cups of the cranberry purée, the 2 tablespoons of lemon juice, and the cassis into the yolks. Fold in the whipped cream, then the whites.

Spoon enough lime sherbet into the soufflé mold or molds to come halfway to the top of the collar. Smooth out the sherbet with the back of a spoon, and tap it down into the mold so that there will be no air bubbles.

Spoon the soufflé mixture on top of the lime sherbet. You can fill the mold to the very top of the collar. Freeze, covered with plastic wrap, for several hours or overnight.

Just before serving, combine the remaining ½ cup cranberry purée with ½ cup cranberry juice cocktail. Press the mixture through a sieve so it will be clear and smooth. Set aside until ready to serve.

To serve, remove foil collar. Spoon a pool of purée on individual plates, then cover with a portion of frozen soufflé.

STRAWBERRY SOUFFLÉ

1 pint strawberries, cleaned and hulled

3 tablespoons strawberry preserves

2 tablespoons imported Kirschwasser (cherry brandy)

4 egg yolks

¼ cup sugar

1 cup heavy cream

4 egg whites

Few drops of lemon juice

Purée the berries in a blender or food processor. Stir in the preserves and the kirsch.

In a large bowl, beat the egg yolks with half the sugar until very thick and light in color.

In a medium bowl, beat the cream until it holds soft peaks.

In another large bowl, beat the egg whites with the lemon juice until foamy, then gradually add remaining sugar, continuing to beat until whites are firm but still glossy.

Fold the berry mixture into the egg yolks. Fold in the whipped cream, then the egg whites. Spoon into 8 individual molds or one 6- or 7-cup mold, cover with plastic wrap, and freeze for several hours or overnight.

CREAM-PUFF SOUFFLÉ WITH HOT FUDGE SAUCE

SERVES 10 TO 12

1 recipe Cream Puffs (page 110)

SOUFFLÉ

6 egg yolks

½ cup sugar

4 egg whites

Few drops of lemon juice

1 cup heavy cream

3 tablespoons Bailey's Irish Cream

2 tablespoons Irish whiskey

HOT FUDGE SAUCE

8 ounces good-quality bittersweet chocolate (Callebaut)

½ cup heavy cream

To make the soufflé, beat the egg yolks with half the sugar in a large bowl until very thick and light in color. Beat the heavy cream until it holds soft peaks.

In another large bowl, beat the whites with the lemon juice until foamy, then gradually add the remaining sugar while continuing to beat until whites are firm but still glossy. Stir the Irish Cream and the whiskey into the yolks, then fold in the whites.

Fill the puffs with the soufflé mixture and replace the tops. Place on cookie sheets or trays, cover with foil, and freeze several hours or overnight.

Just before serving, make the Hot Fudge Sauce. Melt the chocolate with the cream, stirring well to blend. Pass the hot sauce at the table, to be poured over frozen soufflés.

PEAR SOUFFLÉ IN CHOCOLATE CUPS

You can make your own chocolate cups if you're feeling ambitious. If not, specialty grocery stores usually carry them.

SERVES 8

- **10 ounces good-quality bittersweet chocolate, or 8 ready-made chocolate cups**
- **1 (13¾-ounce) can pears, packed in unsweetened juice, drained well and puréed in a blender or food processor**
- **2 tablespoons Pear William (*eau-de-vie de poire*)**
- **1½ tablespoons lemon juice**
- **2 egg yolks**
- **2 tablespoons sugar**
- **½ cup heavy cream**
- **2 egg whites**

If you're making your own chocolate cups, you'll need eight 6-ounce paper or Styrofoam cups. Set them on squares of plastic wrap and pull the wrap up around the outside of the cups so that they are enclosed completely. Tuck the excess wrap into the middle of the cups. The outside should be as smooth as possible.

Break the chocolate into small pieces and put it in the top of a double boiler. Melt the chocolate over barely simmering water and remove when thoroughly melted and just lukewarm.

Dip the plastic-covered cups to about half their height in the lukewarm chocolate, coating the outside of the cups as evenly as possible. As you remove the cups from the chocolate, smooth the bottoms against the inside of the double boiler or with a spatula.

As each cup is dipped, set it down on a piece of parchment paper. When the chocolate is set on all the cups, place them in the refrigerator to chill.

When chilled, pull the excess plastic wrap from the centers and remove the paper cups. You'll have chocolate cups with plastic wrap inside. Gently twist the wrap free, and refrigerate the cups until ready to use.

To make the soufflé, combine the pear purée, Pear William, and all but a few drops of the lemon juice in a medium bowl.

In a large mixing bowl, beat the egg yolks with 1 tablespoon of the sugar until very thick and light in color.

In a medium bowl, whip the cream until it holds stiff peaks.

In a medium bowl, whip the egg whites with the remaining few drops of lemon juice until foamy. Gradually add the remaining tablespoon sugar while continuing to beat until firm but still glossy.

Fold the pear mixture into the egg yolks. Fold in the whipped cream, then fold in the egg whites.

Spoon the soufflé batter into the chocolate cups, smooth the tops, and freeze several hours or overnight.

GRAPEFRUIT SOUFFLÉ IN TULIP CUPS

Grapefruit is one of the unsung heroes of the citrus-dessert world. This soufflé can also be frozen in regular soufflé molds, but its elegance will be greatly enhanced by the tulip cups.

SERVES 8

1 **large grapefruit**

6 **egg yolks**

5 **tablespoons sugar**

1 **cup heavy cream**

3 **egg whites**

Few drops of lemon juice

2 **tablespoons Napoleon Mandarine (mandarin orange liqueur)**

8 **Tulip Cups (page 108)**

Grate the zest of half the grapefruit. Juice the grapefruit. Place three-quarters of the juice in a small, heavy saucepan, and reserve the rest. Add the zest to the pan and bring the mixture to a boil over medium-high heat. Let boil until thick and syrupy, and reduced to about 2 tablespoons. Cool, then add the reserved juice.

In a large mixing bowl, beat the egg yolks with half the sugar until very thick and light in color.

In a medium bowl, whip the cream until it holds soft peaks.

In another medium bowl, beat the egg whites with the lemon juice until foamy. Gradually add the remaining sugar while continuing to beat until whites are stiff but still glossy.

Stir the grapefruit syrup and Napoleon Mandarine into the egg yolks. Fold in the whipped cream, then the egg whites.

Cover and freeze the mixture. To serve, scoop rounded spoonfuls into the prepared tulip cups.

MASTER RECIPES

PASTRY CREAM
(CRÈME PATISSIÈRE)

This rich custard is the basis for the Brownie Soufflé (page 60), but it can also be spread on tart crusts and topped with fresh fruit.

MAKES ABOUT 3 CUPS

2 cups milk

½ cup sugar

¼ cup sifted cake flour

3 eggs

2 egg yolks

Heat the milk just to the boiling point.

Mix the sugar and cake flour in a heavy-bottom saucepan. Whisk in the eggs and egg yolks and incorporate well. Still whisking, add the hot milk very gradually.

Cook the custard over medium heat until it comes to a gentle boil, stirring thoroughly around the bottom and sides of the pan. Boil gently for about 2 minutes.

Pour custard into a bowl and cool at room temperature. To prevent a crust from forming on the custard as it cools, lay plastic wrap directly on the surface. When cool, refrigerate, covered with plastic, until ready to use. The custard will keep for several days.

FLAKY PASTRY DOUGH

MAKES 8 TARTLET SHELLS
3 OR 4 INCHES IN DIAMETER

2¾ cups all-purpose flour

1 teaspoon sugar

Pinch of salt

¾ cup (1½ sticks) unsalted butter

1 egg

3 to 5 tablespoons ice water

Stir together the flour, sugar, and salt in a large mixing bowl. Using the paddle attachment of an electric mixer (or a pastry cutter or a fork), cut in the butter until the mixture resembles cornmeal. With the mixer on low speed, add the egg, then the water a tablespoon at a time, mixing just until the dough begins to mass around the paddle. Do not overbeat.

Gather the dough together into a ball; wrap in wax paper, plastic wrap, or aluminum foil, and chill for 30 minutes.

Preheat the oven to 350° F. Roll out the dough on a floured board to ⅛-inch thickness. Using a biscuit cutter or a very sharp knife, cut circles large enough to fit eight 3- or 4-inch tartlet molds. Without stretching the dough, fit the circles inside the molds and trim the edges.

Lay pieces of aluminum foil over the dough, pressing to conform to the tartlet shape. Fill with uncooked rice and/or dried beans, and bake for about 10 minutes.

Remove the foil and rice and/or beans (save them for the next time you bake), and continue baking until shells are lightly browned and baked through.

NOTE: Leftover dough may be wrapped tightly in aluminum foil and plastic wrap and frozen for several weeks. Let thaw in refrigerator before using.

SWEET PASTRY DOUGH

MAKES EIGHT 3- OR 4-INCH
CRISP-CRUSTED PASTRY SHELLS

½ cup (1 stick) unsalted butter, softened

½ cup sugar

6 tablespoons finely ground almonds

½ teaspoon grated lime zest

1 egg

2 cups all-purpose flour

3 to 5 tablespoons ice water

In a large bowl of an electric mixer, combine the butter, sugar, almonds, and lime zest. Using the paddle attachment at low speed, beat the mixture until it has the texture of cornmeal. Still on low speed, beat in the egg. Add the flour all at once, mixing until just incorporated. Add only enough water to make the dough hold together, working the dough as little as possible at this point.

Gather the dough into a ball, flatten slightly, and wrap in wax paper. Refrigerate until ready to use.

To bake, preheat the oven to 350° F. Roll the dough out on a floured board to ⅛-inch thickness. Using a biscuit cutter or a very sharp knife, cut circles large enough to fit eight 3- or 4-inch tartlet molds. Without stretching the dough, fit the circles inside the molds and trim the edges.

Lay pieces of aluminum foil over the dough, pressing to conform to the tartlet shape. Fill with uncooked rice and/or dried beans, and bake for about 10 minutes. Remove the foil and rice and/or beans (save them for the next time you bake), and continue baking until the shells are lightly browned and baked through.

NOTE: This recipe can be multiplied up to 5 times. The dough will keep in the freezer, divided into quantities most useful to you and wrapped tightly in plastic wrap and foil, for several weeks. Let thaw in refrigerator before using.

SPONGE CAKE
(GENOISE)

This is a basic French butter sponge cake. The recipe provides more than enough cake for the soufflés requiring them. Leftover cake can be frozen.

MAKES A 9 × 13-INCH CAKE

½ cup (1 stick) unsalted butter

6 eggs

1 cup sugar

1 teaspoon vanilla extract

1 cup sifted cake flour

Preheat the oven to 350° F. Butter and flour a 9 × 13-inch cake pan.

Melt the butter in a small saucepan over low heat. When the butter is completely liquid, skim the foam off the top with a small spoon, being careful not to disturb the milky residue on the bottom. Pour off the clear butter into another small pot, and discard the milky residue. Keep the butter lukewarm.

Whisk together the eggs, sugar, and vanilla in a large mixing bowl. Fill a large pan with enough hot water to come at least 2 inches up the sides of the bowl and place over low heat. Put the bowl in the pan and whisk the mixture with the whisk attachment of an electric mixer or a hand whisk until it triples in volume and feels cool to the touch.

Remove the bowl from the pan. Using a rubber spatula, fold in one-third of the flour, followed by one-third of the butter. Repeat twice more until all the flour and butter are added. Don't overwork the batter at this point or the cake will be tough and dry.

Pour the batter into the prepared pan and bake for 20 to 25 minutes, or until the top is lightly browned and the cake pulls away slightly from the sides of the pan. Let cool for about 5 minutes, then invert on a rack to cool completely.

CRÊPES

3 cups milk

6 eggs

3 cups all-purpose flour

2 tablespoons sugar

½ cup (1 stick) unsalted butter, melted and cooled

Milk (optional)

Additional melted butter for cooking

Combine milk, eggs, flour, and sugar in a blender or food processor, and blend on low speed until no lumps remain in the flour. Add the butter and blend another few seconds. Refrigerate the batter for at least 30 minutes before using.

When ready to use, the batter should be about as thick as heavy cream. If it has thickened too much after refrigeration, whisk in a little milk.

To cook the crêpes, heat a 6- or 8-inch nonstick frying pan or crêpe pan over medium-high heat. Brush with a thin layer of butter. When the pan is thoroughly heated, whisk the batter briefly, then with a ladle or measuring cup pour in enough (about ¼ cup) to cover the bottom of the pan. Rotate and tilt the pan as you pour to evenly distribute the batter.

Cook until the crêpe begins to look dry around the

edges and bubbles have formed on the top, about 1 minute. Turn the crêpe over, using a spatula to loosen if it's stuck in places (in a nonstick pan the first crêpe or so might do this). Cook just until the underside is brown, about another 30 seconds. Continue cooking the crêpes, brushing the pan again with butter if necessary.

As the crêpes are cooked, stack them on a plate with a layer of wax paper between each.

NOTE: This recipe can be cut in half.

TULIP CUPS

MAKES 12 CUPS

¾ **cup plus 2 tablespoons confectioners' sugar**

7 tablespoons unsalted butter, softened

3 egg whites

½ **cup plus 1 tablespoon all-purpose flour**

1 egg yolk

Preheat the oven to 475° F. Grease a 14 × 17-inch cookie sheet.

Combine the confectioners' sugar and butter in a large mixing bowl. Mix well by hand or use the lowest speed of an electric mixer. Don't beat hard. Mix in the egg whites, then add the flour. Finally, mix in the egg yolks. The idea is to thoroughly incorporate all the ingredients without working the dough too much.

For each tulip, spread 1 heaping tablespoon of batter onto the cookie sheet, forming a 6-inch circle the same thickness all around. Leave 2 inches between circles.

Bake about 3½ to 4 minutes, until the cookies are dry and the edges brown. At this point you need to work quickly because all the tulip cups must be formed while the cookies are still warm. Keeping the cookie sheet on the open oven door while you work will help. Using a wide spatula, remove 1 cookie from the baking sheet and immediately drape it over the bottom of a drinking glass. Gently press the overhanging parts of the cookie against the sides of the glass, folding a bit where necessary.

Remove the cookie from the glass and repeat the process. If the cookies cool too quickly to form, reheat them for a few seconds in the oven before proceeding.

Store in an airtight container, unrefrigerated but in a cool place. The cookies will collapse if they're exposed to humidity.

CREAM PUFFS

This recipe can be made ahead and frozen. Cream Puffs make fine containers for various sweet and savory fillings.

MAKES APPROXIMATELY 12 PUFFS

1 **cup water**

½ **cup (1 stick) unsalted butter**

1⅓ **cups all-purpose flour**

6 **eggs**

Preheat the oven to 400° F.

Put the water and butter in a medium saucepan, and set over medium-high heat. Adjust the heat so that the butter is melted about the same time as the water begins to boil. Off the heat, add the flour all at once and stir until blended. Over medium-high heat, beat the mixture until it forms a mass around the spoon and a film begins to form on the bottom and sides of the pan. This indicates the flour is cooked.

Add the eggs one at a time, beating well after each addition. You can use an electric mixer for this. The batter should be shiny and fall slightly from a spoon when lifted.

Using a pastry bag fitted with a ½-inch plain tip (or a spoon), form 3- to 4-inch mounds of dough on a greased cookie sheet, leaving 2 inches between each. Bake for 15 minutes. Lower the oven to 350° F. and bake another 10 minutes, or until the puffs are browned and dry-looking. Let cool on the sheet.

When cool, cut the tops off the puffs and carefully pull out any uncooked parts from the inside. Place tops back on the cream puffs. At this point, the puffs can be used immediately or frozen for later use.

CRÈME ANGLAISE

2 cups milk

5 egg yolks

½ cup sugar

Bring the milk to a boil in a 2-quart saucepan over medium-high heat.

In a medium bowl, beat the egg yolks with the sugar until very thick and light in color.

Gradually pour about 1 cup of the hot milk into the yolks, whisking as you pour. Return the mixture to the saucepan and stir over low heat until thick enough to coat a wooden spoon. To test, dip the spoon in the custard, then run your finger through the custard on the spoon. The division made by your finger should remain.

Immediately remove from the heat and whisk to cool. Refrigerate, well covered, until ready to use. It will keep for 2 or 3 days.

VARIATIONS

CALVADOS SAUCE: add Calvados (apple brandy) to taste.

MOCHA SAUCE: Dissolve 2 tablespoons instant espresso powder in 2 tablespoons of dark rum. Stir into Crème Anglaise.

RASPBERRY COULIS

This is simple to make and excellent on ice cream, but really perfect with the Nougat Glacé (page 84).

MAKES APPROXIMATELY 1 CUP

2 cartons (approximately 1 pint) fresh raspberries or 1 10-ounce box frozen raspberries (preferably without sugar), thawed

Sugar

Lemon juice

Purée the raspberries in a food processor, then put through a sieve to remove the seeds. Add the sugar and lemon juice to taste and stir to blend. Chill before serving.

NOUGATINE

2½ cups sugar

2 tablespoons light corn syrup

½ cup water

3 cups sliced almonds

Put the sugar, corn syrup, and water in a heavy 3-quart saucepan. Stir until well combined. Put the saucepan over medium heat. As it cooks, wash down the inside edges of the pan with a pastry brush repeatedly dipped in cold water. This will rinse away any undissolved sugar crystals that might begin a chain reaction leading to a crystalized mess in the saucepan.

Stir until the sugar comes to a boil, then stop. When the sugar is boiling, gently agitate the pan to distribute heat evenly. Watch the pan carefully and remove it from the heat when you begin to see small puffs of smoke coming from the sugar; it should be dark brown but not burned.

Add the almonds and stir quickly, then pour the hot caramelized sugar onto a well-oiled 11 × 15-inch jelly-roll pan. Let it cool. Nougat can be kept well wrapped at room temperature for at least a week, and can be kept longer if dry and well wrapped.

When ready to use, turn the nougat into nougatine by putting it in a sturdy plastic bag and bashing it with a hammer or heavy mallet. You should end up with small pieces, not dust.

ACKNOWLEDGMENTS

For as long as I can remember I have loved everything about pastries and desserts. As a child my favorite Golden Book was about a French poodle named Pierre, a pastry chef whose shop was filled with pastel-colored petits fours. I was enchanted. I never dreamed that I would have the chance to work in a professional kitchen and to prepare the fantasies of my childhood. And without those opportunities and experiences, I would not have come to write this book.

I would like to thank the late Anne Crutcher, food editor of the *Washington Daily News* and *Washington Star*, who ordered the first wedding cake I ever made; Phyllis Richman, food editor of the *Washington Post*, whose enthusiasm and encouragement made me move into the "real kitchens"; Barbara Witt of the Big Cheese Restaurant, who gave me my first chance; Deirdre Pierce and Patricia Altobello, food writers, who always appreciated; Patrick Musel, pastry chef of Washington's finest pastry shop, who taught me so many techniques and who shared so much of his knowledge; Roland Mesnier, pastry chef of the White House, who gave me a valuable year as his pastry assistant; Joan Nathan, food writer for the *New York Times* and cookbook author, who has always believed in my work, and who steered Richard and me in the right direction; George Lang, who is everything to the food world, and who paved the way for us at Clarkson N. Potter; Lisa Yockelson, food writer, cookbook author, and baker *extraordinaire*, whose generosity and way with words helped us move on; Nancy Novogrod, former editor, who started the ball rolling; and Shirley Wohl, our editor, who stepped in and caught the ball with such grace.

I would also like to thank Richard Chirol, whose ideas and inspiration made this book happen; Linda Greider, food writer for *Washingtonian* magazine, for her never-ending help in testing recipes and pulling everything together; Jay and Dan Amernick, my sons, who put up with late dinners, messy kitchens, and so much more, and who, with unflagging humor, always put a smile on my face; and Lincoln Mudd, whose unfailing support and endless kindnesses got me through the hard times.

A.A.

I would like to thank my father, Guy Chirol, a *confiseur*, who taught me how to make a glacéed strawberry, at the very least; my two teachers at the Chambre de Commerce in Paris, Jean Marie Brossier and the late André Tranchant; my chef and friend Jean Louis Palladin, for the many techniques he taught me; Jean Louis Brochard, who gave me the opportunity to come to the United States; Fredy Girardet, for the original soufflé recipe; Phyllis Richman, whose understanding of my work did not go unappreciated; and Ann Amernick, my partner in this writing experience.

R.C.

INDEX